IRELAND

LANDMARKS, LANDSCAPES & HIDDEN TREASURES

Publisher and Creative Director: Nick Wells
Project Editor: Cat Taylor
Picture Research and Editorial: Josie Mitchell
Art Director: Mike Spender
Digital Design and Production: Chris Herbert

Special thanks to: Frances Bodiam, Katherine Mills, Laura Bulbeck, Sarah Goulding,
Amanda Leigh, Victoria Lyle, Melinda Révèsz, Gemma Walters and Polly Prior

FLAME TREE PUBLISHING

Crabtree Hall, Crabtree Lane
Fulham, London SW6 6TY
United Kingdom

www.flametreepublishing.com

First published 2015

19 17 15 16 18
1 3 5 7 9 10 8 6 4 2

A CIP record for this book is available from the British Library.

ISBN: 978-1-78361-423-3

Printed in Singapore

IRELAND

LANDMARKS, LANDSCAPES & HIDDEN TREASURES

Text by Kevin Eyres and Michael Kerrigan

FLAME TREE
PUBLISHING

Contents

Introduction 10

Ulster North **16**

Dunagree Point, Inishowen, Donegal 20

Doagh Famine Village, Inishowen, Donegal 20

Folk Museum, Glencolumbkille, Donegal 24

Portsalon, Fanad Peninsula, Donegal 24

Fanad Peninsula, Near Rathmullan, Donegal 28

Mulroy Bay, Fanad Peninsula, Donegal...................28

Guildhall, Londonderry City, Londonderry 32

Reconciliation Monument, Londonderry City,

    Londonderry 32

Mussenden Temple, Londonderry 36

Near Portstewart, Londonderry 36

Coast, Near Portrush, Antrim 40

Dunluce Castle, Antrim 40

Dunseverick Castle, Antrim 44

Giant's Causeway, Antrim 44

Carrick-a-Rede, Antrim 48

Glens of Antrim, Antrim 48

Belfast City Hall, Antrim 52

Windmill, Near Millisle, Down 52

Scrabo Tower, Near Newtownards, Down...............56

Mount Stewart House, Down 56

Hillsborough Castle, Down 60

Waterfall, Crawfordsburn Country Park, Down 60

Mourne Mountains, Newcastle, Down 64

Mourne Mountains, Down 64

The Silent Valley and Ben Crom, Down.................68

Ulster South **70**

Ballykeel Dolmen, Armagh 74

St Patrick's Cathedral, Armagh City, Armagh 74

Beaghmore Stone Circles, Near Cookstown,

    Tyrone 78

Ulster History Park, Near Omagh, Tyrone 78

Sperrin Mountains, Tyrone 82

Enniskillen Castle, Fermanagh 82

Devenish Island, Lower Lough Erne, Fermanagh ..86

Hilton Park, Monaghan 86

Connacht North **90**

Monastic Ruins, Inishmurray Island, Sligo 94

Classiebawn Castle, Mullaghmore, Sligo 94

Ben Bulben, Sligo 98

River Garavogue, Sligo City, Sligo 98

Markree Castle, Collooney, Sligo 102

Parkes Castle, Lough Gill, Leitrim 102

Glencar Waterfall, Leitrim 106

Connacht South **108**

Boyle Abbey, Roscommon 112

Castle Island, Lough Key Forest Park, Boyle,.............

Roscommon 112

Lily Pool and Temple, Strokestown Park,

Roscommon 116

Kylemore, Galway 116

Bunowen Bay and Twelve Pins,

Connemara, Galway...............................120

Derryclare Lough, Connemara, Galway 120

Dogs Bay, Near Roundstone, Connemara, Galway .. 124

Galway City, Galway 124

Dunguaire Castle, Kinvara, Galway........................ 128

Dun Aengus Fort, Inishmore, Aran Islands,

Galway 128

Leinster North **132**

River Shannon, Athlone Town, Westmeath 136

Traditional Pub, Moate, Westmeath 136

Burial Chamber and Standing Stone,

    Newgrange, Meath 140

Trim Castle, Trim, Meath 140

Birr Castle, Offaly 144

The Abbey at Clonmacnoise, Offaly 144

Sculpture of Jim Larkin and the Spire,

    O'Connell Street, Dublin 148

River Liffey, Dublin...148

O'Connell Street, Dublin 152

Trinity College, Dublin 152

Dublin Castle, Dublin 156

The Four Courts, Dublin 156

The Dail, Government Buildings, Dublin 160

Custom House, River Liffey, Dublin 160

Ha'penny Bridge, Dublin 164

Christ Church Cathedral, Dublin 164

Leinster South **168**

Pleached Lime Alley, Heywood Gardens, Laois 172

Stradbally, Laois 172

St Joseph's Square, Maynooth College, Kildare......176

River Liffey, Wicklow 176

Wicklow Mountains, Wicklow 180

Powerscourt Gardens, Wicklow 180

Glendalough, Wicklow 184

Glendalough, Wicklow Mountains, Wicklow 184

Kilkenny Castle, Kilkenny 188

River Barrow, At Graiguenamanagh, Kilkenny ..188

Kilmore Quay, Wexford 192

Booley Bay, Hook Peninsula, Wexford 192

Hook Head, Wexford 196

Munster North **198**

Poulnabrone Dolmen, The Burren, Clare 202

Cliffs of Moher, Clare 202

Adare, Limerick 206

Rock of Cashel, Tipperary 206

Cahir Castle, Tipperary 210

The Swiss Cottage, Near Cahir, Tipperary 210

Holy Cross Abbey, Near Thurles,Tipperary 214

Munster South...**216**

Annascaul, The Dingle Peninsula, Kerry 220

Slea Head, The Dingle Peninsula, Kerry 220

Lough Currane, Waterville, Kerry 224

Derrynane Bay, Deenish & Scariff Islands,

    Kerry 224

Sneem Sculpture Park, Kerry 228

Sneem, Ring of Kerry, Kerry 228

Torc Waterfall, Ring of Kerry, Kerry 232

Waterville, Ring of Kerry, Kerry 232

Allihies, Beara Peninsula, Cork 236

Garinish Island, Cork 236

Blarney Castle, Cork 240

Red Strand and Galley Head, Cork 240

Cobh Cathedral, Cork 244

Lismore Castle, Waterford 244

Burial Site of Samuel Grubb, Knockmealdown

    Mountains, Waterford 248

Dungarvan, Near Waterford, Waterford 248

Spraoi Festival, Waterford City, Waterford 252

Acknowledgements **254**

Index..**255**

Introduction

May the road rise to meet you.
May the wind be always at your back.
May the sun shine warm upon your face.
And rains fall soft upon your fields.

(Anon)

IRELAND is the land of great heroes and heroines, of myths and legends, monumental castles and elegant country houses, of gentle rain and lush green pastures, of towering cliffs, tranquil river estuaries and magnificent lakes. It has been home to Fionn MacCul (Finn MacCool) and Cúchulainn, James Joyce and Brendan Behan, Jonathan Swift and W. B. Yeats, George Bernard Shaw and Oscar Wilde.

Perhaps we should define what we mean by Ireland. The 32 counties that make up the third largest island in Europe are currently divided into the Republic of Ireland (Eire), and Northern Ireland: one of the four countries of the United Kingdom. The story that led to this division is, as we shall see, a long one and has shaped much of the country's turbulent history. However, the Ireland of this book is one land: the emerald isle that sits at Europe's most westerly point, forming a bulwark against the might of the Atlantic Ocean.

To appreciate the secrets of Ireland we have to know something of its history. Only by being aware of Ireland's past can we start to understand the importance of the enduring relationship that the people of Ireland have had with their country and how this has shaped, and continues to shape, both themselves and their island.

Ireland's modern history, which begins with the arrival of the Celts in 700 BC, has been one of turmoil, invasion, occupation and assimilation. As a small island divided into smaller, often-warring, kingdoms, Ireland was prey to opportunistic invaders, and almost continual internal conflict. Finally, with the arrival of St Patrick and Christianity in the fifth century, came three centuries of relative calm and prosperity. This golden age was itself ended by the arrival of increasingly large forces of marauding Vikings from AD 790 onwards.

The Vikings, lured by the wealth of the many Christian monasteries that flourished throughout the country, soon established themselves in Ireland and built fortified settlements at what are now Dublin, Waterford, Cork and Limerick. Following Brian Boru's decisive defeat of their forces in 1014, many Vikings remained, adopting the language, laws and culture of the native Celtic population.

This pattern of invasion and assimilation, rather than outright colonisation, continued with the arrival of the Anglo-Normans in 1169. In the fourteenth century, the English Crown

sought to re-establish the division between the native Irish and the Anglo-Normans by introducing the draconian Statutes of Kilkenny. These laws attempted to prohibit the growth of the Irish language and culture, banning intermarriage and even forbidding native-born Irish from entering walled towns. In spite of these measures, the Anglo-Normans continued to adopt the indigenous Gaelic culture. The English Reformation of 1530, and the subsequent dissolution of the monasteries in 1536, changed everything.

Henry VIII's break with Rome, and the establishment of the Protestant Church in England, added a religious element to the political mix that was to reverberate down the centuries, and even in the twenty-first century has yet to be resolved. During the reigns of Elizabeth I and James I, the policy of Plantations was introduced. Lands and estates were confiscated from the native Catholic Irish and given to Protestant English (and later Scottish) immigrants. A brief period of Irish independence after the 1641 rebellion was followed by Cromwell's brutal re-assertion of English rule in 1652. These early dreams of home rule were finally crushed at the Battle of the Boyne in 1690.

Over the next century, the Protestant colonisers themselves became part of Irish society and began to lobby England for greater independence. More alarmingly for the English, a number of radical movements were springing up demanding greater rights for the downtrodden Catholic majority, including the right to vote. Limited Catholic emancipation was finally achieved in 1829, but the cynical and uncaring reaction of the English and Anglo-Irish landlords to the suffering of the Catholic Irish during the terrible potato famines of 1845–49 led to much more widespread radical republicanism. At the same time, Gladstone's attempts to introduce Home Rule led the increasingly Protestant northeast of Ireland to organize and lobby against what they feared would be the loss of the political and economic advantages they had been granted by the English over the previous two centuries.

Events moved swiftly in the early part of the twentieth century. The Home Rule Act was passed in 1914, despite trenchant opposition from Ulster Protestants, only to be immediately suspended by the outbreak of the First World War. The 1916 Easter Uprising in Dublin, an abortive attempt to wrestle power from the English, was followed in 1919 by the unilateral declaration of an Irish Republic containing all the 32 counties. This led to another brutal Anglo-Irish War that culminated in the Anglo-Irish Treaty of 1921. The treaty was a compromise that replaced the Irish Republic with an Irish Free State but that allowed the six counties of Northern Ireland the option of opting out, which they immediately did.

At this point the Irish were fatally split between those who thought the Treaty too much of a compromise, and those who thought the deal was the best they could achieve at the time. A bloody and bitter civil war ensued with the pro-treaty faction finally defeating the anti-treaty Irish Republican Army (IRA). The implications of this tumultuous period – almost a century ago – are still being felt today. The Irish Republic's two main parties,

Fianna Fáil and Fine Gael, are the direct descendants of the two factions that fought out that tragic conflict.

The Irish Free State finally became the Republic of Ireland in 1949 when it left the British Commonwealth. Today the six counties of Northern Ireland remain part of the United

Kingdom. Northern Ireland's painful recent history is part of a sequence of events that stretches back to the Plantations of the sixteenth century and further back to the Anglo-Norman invasions of the twelfth century.

It can be easy to forget that behind the laid-back pace of life and the easy-going, hospitable nature of the Irish lies a turbulent, violent history. It is an enduring testament both to the Irish character and its culture that they have survived so harsh a history intact. As Sigmund Freud memorably remarked, "This is one race of people for whom psychoanalysis is of no use whatsoever".

Ireland's resolute struggle to maintain its own Gaelic culture in the face of successive waves of invaders has left a rich legacy not only in its monuments but also in its literature and its music. You can see this most clearly in the Irish-speaking *Gaeltacht* regions of the western counties, but throughout Ireland you will never be far away from powerful reminders of the genuine connection that the Irish feel for their rich oral and musical traditions.

Although Eire is nowadays a thriving and influential member of the European Union, with a booming economy and the sobriquet 'Celtic Tiger', it is still a largely rural nation.

Northern Ireland is also flourishing and, though traditionally more industrialized than the Republic, it is also for the most part rural. The Industrial Revolution, which caused so much upheaval in nineteenth-century England, did have an impact on the area around Belfast but bypassed the rest of Ireland almost entirely, leaving it largely unspoilt by urban blight and industrial decay even today.

The physical landscape of Ireland is a combination of the wild and rugged and the pastoral. In essence the topography is one of a dramatic coastline surrounding a less spectacular, albeit lushly beautiful, central plain. However, Ireland certainly manages to contain a remarkable variety of terrain within its relatively small area, from the towering cliffs of Slieve League in Donegal, to the rich pastures and raised bogs of Roscommon, and the serene lakes of Fermanagh. The 32 counties of Ireland offer a variety of unforgettable scenery that provides a fitting backdrop for the turmoil of its history, the wealth of its historic monuments and the warm, civilized nature of its people.

Ireland is traditionally divided into four provinces, historically referred to as kingdoms – Ulster, Connacht, Leinster, and Munster. A fifth province, Meath, now forms part of Leinster. To make your journey through the book easier, we have divided each of the four provinces into north and south regions.

As you explore the wonderfully evocative images that follow, remember that the beauty of Ireland is not the twee attractiveness of picture-postcard clichés, but the product of the visceral and often painful history of a proud and cultured people, and of their enduring love for their beautiful island.

Ulster North

Although today most people associate Ulster solely with Northern Ireland, ours is the Ulster of the four Kingdoms of Ireland and so includes three counties from Northern Ireland and one, Donegal, from the Republic.

If the reporting of the 'Troubles' has shaped your impressions of Northern Ireland, you risk ignoring one of the most beautiful regions in the whole of Europe. The north coast can vie with anywhere in Ireland for breathtaking scenery. In County Down, where St Patrick first landed and where he lies buried, the Mountains of Mourne really do 'sweep down to the sea' revealing a coastline of golden beaches and picturesque fishing villages.

All the quiet beauty of County Antrim with its fertile green glens and wonderfully preserved Norman castles is overshadowed by the sheer spectacle of the Giant's Causeway, one of the great natural wonders of the world.

As the green fields and pastures of Londonderry merge into the wild mountains and rugged coastline of Donegal, the scenery changes again. Bearing the full brunt of the Atlantic, the towering cliffs of Slieve League are among the highest and most dramatic in Europe.

The north of Ulster is a wonderful introduction to the variety of riches that the whole of Ireland has to offer.

Dunagree Point
INISHOWEN, DONEGAL

Right. Vessels leaving the shelter of Lough Foyle for the open waters of the Atlantic have to run the gauntlet of the rockbound coast around Inishowen. Many ships were lost here before, in 1837, a pair of lighthouses were built on Dunagree Point. Only the more westerly of these survives: the other was sadly demolished in 1961. In this part of Donegal we are reminded of the eccentricities of Irish political geography. Standing here, in the 'South', we are at a higher latitude than we would be just about anywhere in the 'North'.

Doagh Famine Village
INISHOWEN, DONEGAL

Next page. The Great Famine of the 1840s was a humanitarian disaster: about a million people died of hunger and disease. A similar number were forced to emigrate. The immediate cause of the tragedy was the *Phytophthora infestans*, the potato blight. But official attitudes also played their part. Ireland was exporting food throughout the crisis, even as its people starved. The suffering and disruption the episode caused was to leave a permanent mark on the Irish identity and the Irish scene. The Doagh Famine Village is at once a monument and an enthralling outdoor museum.

Folk Museum
GLENCOLUMBKILLE, DONEGAL

Right. Glencolumbkille, named after Saint Columba, is in the middle of the *Gaeltacht* (Irish speaking) region of south Donegal. Situated by a fine sandy beach at the end of a lushly fertile glen, this delightfully understated folk museum is set in a group of small farmhouses and barns. Among its exhibits is a replica of a National School and, more intriguingly, a shebeen where locally brewed and untaxed liquor was sold, away from the attention of the Revenue men.

Portsalon
FANAD PENINSULA, DONEGAL

Next page. The north coast of Donegal has two great sea loughs, Lough Foyle and Lough Swilly. The Fanan Peninsula forms the western shore of Lough Swilly and its cliff-edge lighthouse bears testimony to the dangers of the wild coast and the power of the Atlantic. Portsalon, a sheltered spot at the mouth of the lough, was once a thriving seaside resort. Sadly it has lost its allure for holidaymakers, but its wonderful golden strand remains facing east towards the Inishowen Peninsula and Malin Head.

Fanad Peninsula
NEAR RATHMULLAN, DONEGAL

Right. Further inland on the Fanad Peninsula, away from the rugged coastline, the countryside has a more pastoral air. Cows graze in green pastures in the shadow of gentle hills, while white clouds scud across the blue sky. Rathmullen itself is a pretty little seaside town, its houses tracing the gentle arc of the bay. Nearby is Rathmelton, an elegant Plantation town, founded in the seventeenth century as a base for incoming English colonisers.

Mulroy Bay
FANAD PENINSULA, DONEGAL

Next page. Under a beautiful sunset a boat sits calmly at anchor in the unruffled waters of Mulroy Bay, an outstandingly beautiful marine inlet between the Fanad and Rosguill Peninsulas on Donegal's north coast. Although the inlet is little more than 350 m (1,155 ft) wide in places, driving between the two shores at the coast involves a journey of some 50 km (31 miles). For this reason, Mulroy Bay is soon to be spanned by a landmark bridge with a clearance height of 20 m (66 ft).

Guildhall
LONDONDERRY CITY, LONDONDERRY

Right. Londonderry's Guildhall stands resplendent in the Spring sunshine. Standing just outside the massive city walls, the Guildhall's neo-Gothic elegance is a tribute to the wealth and influence of Londonderry in the late nineteenth century when the Guildhall was built. It survived being damaged by a serious fire in 1908 and being bombed in 1972, and has now been restored to its original glory, acting as a civic and cultural centre for the people of the city.

Reconciliation Monument
LONDONDERRY CITY, LONDONDERRY

Next page. Craigavon Bridge crosses the River Foyle, connecting Londonderry's mainly Catholic Cityside with the predominantly Protestant Waterside. At the end of the bridge, a bronze statue rises optimistically above the traffic. Maurice Harron's sculpture Hands Across the Divide shows two young men standing on separate raised stone platforms, reaching out so that their fingertips can just touch across the gap. It signifies the genuine desire to bridge the divide that has existed in this part of Ireland for many hundreds of years.

Mussenden Temple
LONDONDERRY

Right. The flamboyant eighteenth-century Earl of Bristol, Frederick Hervey, created an estate at Downhill not far from Castlerock to the north of Londonderry. Hervey spent a fortune on the house and gardens, erecting a series of neo-classical buildings in the grounds including the windswept Mussenden Temple, perched precariously on the clifftops. The temple was modelled on the Temple of Vesta at Tivoli near Rome and was originally designed as a library, though some say its real purpose was as a discreet rendezvous for romantic assignations.

Near Portstewart
LONDONDERRY

Next page. The elegant little town of Portstewart with its sheltered harbour was a popular resort with well-heeled Victorians. The town is named after the Scottish Stewart clan who built the town's first house. Such were the pretensions of the locals that the railway station was deliberately built a mile out of the town, to discourage the presence of riff-raff. From the town runs a series of impressive cliff walks overlooking the magnificent three-mile long Portstewart strand, now under the protection of the National Trust.

Coast
NEAR PORTRUSH, ANTRIM

Right. Just along the coast, in County Antrim, is Portstewart's somewhat brasher neighbour, Portrush. Situated on Ranmore Head, Portrush is a lively resort, not afraid to let its hair down. It has a world-class seaside golf course and, like Portstewart, a splendid beach. Walk along the strand and you will be rewarded at the end of your promenade with the impressive site of White Rocks. These limestone cliffs have been fashioned into arches and caves by the relentless force of the wind and waves.

Dunluce Castle
ANTRIM

Next page. Built in the thirteenth century by Richard de Burgh, Earl of Ulster, the roofless ruins of Dunluce Castle stand imperious on the edge of a 30 m (100 ft) basalt cliff. The various local warring clans coveted control of such a strategically sited castle. In 1584, the MacDonnells captured the castle and used booty from a Spanish Armada fleet treasure ship – which ran aground nearby – to modernize it. However, when subsidence tipped the kitchens into the sea during a dinner in 1639, the castle was abandoned.

Dunseverick Castle
ANTRIM

Right. Little more than a ruined tower on a grassy promontory is all that survives of historic Dunseverick Castle. The original castle, built in 1525 BC, was the capital of the ancient Celtic kingdom of Dál Riata, and was directly linked by royal road to Tara, the mythical seat of the High Kings of Ireland. The ruins we see here are part of a later castle built by the MacDonnell clan in the sixteenth century and destroyed by Scottish forces in 1641.

Giant's Causeway
ANTRIM

Next page. It is easy to see why our ancestors thought that the forty thousand regular, mostly hexagonal, basalt columns that make up the Giant's Causeway were more likely to be the work of mythical characters than the volcanic action that actually formed them. According to one legend, the great Irish hero Fionn MacCul (Finn MacCool) built the causeway to bring his love, a female giant who lived on the Hebridean island of Staffa, to his home in Ulster.

Carrick-a-Rede
ANTRIM

Right. Those emboldened by a trip to the Giant's Causeway may want to test their heroic potential by walking across the rope bridge at nearby Carrick-a-Rede. This rather rudimentary structure is the only land access to a salmon fishery located on a tiny island just offshore. The twisting, flexing bridge spans some 20 m (66 ft) and hangs 25 m (83 ft) above the water. Crossing over to the island and back is a daunting prospect even allowing for the safety nets and robust handrails.

Glens of Antrim
ANTRIM

Next page. Over thousands of years, nine rivers carved the deep valleys that form the Nine Glens of Antrim. In the eighteenth century, this Gaelic speaking area was so wild and remote that the Plantations didn't touch it. Today, each of the glens has its own distinct character, from the Alpine charm of Glengariff to the wildness of Glendun. The 'capital' of the Nine Glens is the delightful village of Cushendall, where three glens meet on their way to the sea.

Windmill
NEAR MILLISLE, DOWN

Right. County Down has traditionally been a major centre for grain growing in Ireland, and windmills have been a feature of the landscape here since the eighteenth century. At one point there were over 100 working windmills in the county, though today only a few remain. The Ballycopeland Windmill, a mile west of the seaside resort of Millisle, is the only fully working mill to survive, having been restored to its original condition by the state as a heritage site.

Belfast City Hall
ANTRIM

Next page. A centre for shipbuilding, engineering and textile manufacture, towards the end of the nineteenth century Belfast was becoming one of the kingdom's most important industrial centres. In 1888, the town became a city when it received a royal charter from Queen Victoria. It was then that leaders of the business community and local officialdom started making plans for a city hall worthy of Belfast and its aspirations: this magnificent building in the Renaissance style was the result. The ornamental gardens around it are attractively laid out, a pleasant place to walk and talk in clement weather.

Scrabo Tower

NEAR NEWTOWNARDS, DOWN

Right. Stately Scrabo Tower stands sentinel over Scrabo County Park. It was built in the 1850s as a memorial to Charles Stewart, third Marquis of Londonderry, who worked to help the victims of Ireland's terrible potato famine. The tower overlooks woodlands and disused quarries, where Scrabo stone was dug out and used locally as a building material. Greyabbey Monastery and Belfast's Albert Clock were both built using it, and in the early nineteenth century Scrabo stone was shipped to Dublin and even as far as New York.

Mount Stewart House

DOWN

Next page. Although Mount Stewart House, on the east shore of Lough Strangford, is a fascinating building in its own right, it is the magnificent gardens surrounding the house that have made Mount Stewart internationally famous. Home to the Earls of Londonderry since the eighteenth century, the grounds were laid out in the 1920s by Edith, Lady Londonderry, the wife of the seventh marquis. Today, the 40 hectares (98 acres) of gardens are recognized as a World Heritage Site.

Hillsborough Castle

DOWN

Right. Elegant Hillsborough Castle, originally built in 1650 by Colonel Arthur Hill to maintain control of the strategic Dublin to Carrickfergus road, now plays an important role in relations between Northern Ireland and the mainland. As well as being the official residence of the Queen when in the province, it is also the official residence of the Secretary of State for Northern Ireland. On the international stage, Hillsborough is best known as the place where the historic 1985 Anglo-Irish Agreement was signed.

Waterfall

CRAWFORDSBURN COUNTRY PARK, DOWN

Next page. This attractive waterfall stands at the head of the glen in Crawfordsburn County Park, a delightful estate running along over two miles of Down's rugged coastline. As well as the waterfall, the park includes woodland, meadows, an elegant railway viaduct and a little village of whitewashed houses. Remarkably for an estate that was originally gifted to Scottish Presbyterians, it also contains the aptly named Old Inn that dates from 1614 and is said to be the oldest in Ireland.

Mourne Mountains
NEWCASTLE, DOWN

Right. Newcastle is the largest of County Down's many seaside resorts, spreading along the north coast of Dundrum Bay. It was on the bay's fine sandy beaches that Brunel's *Great Britain* was wrecked in 1846, later to be salvaged and restored. Behind the town rises the impressive bulk of Slieve Donard, which at 850 m (2,800 ft) is Ulster's highest peak. But for many visitors it is the Royal, County Down, a links golf course with a world-class reputation, that makes Newcastle such an attractive spot.

Mourne Mountains
DOWN

Next page. Of all the songs and laments written by homesick Irish emigrants far from home, it is 'The Mountains of Mourne' that remains the best known and closest to many Irish hearts. Percy French, a Roscommon man, composed the song in 1896 in collaboration with his musical partner, Houston Collisson. Before becoming a professional musician and performer, French had been an engineer and for seven years had the somewhat less glamorous occupation of County Cavan's Inspector of Drains.

The Silent Valley and Ben Crom
DOWN

Right. Although the calm stillness of the Silent Valley and Ben Crom seems almost prehistoric, these two lakes in the heart of the Mourne Mountains bear the imprint of very recent human intervention. In the early twentieth century, a dam and huge reservoir were built in the Silent Valley to serve the growing need of Belfast and the rest of County Down for fresh water. In 1957 a further dam and artificial lake were contructed nearby at Ben Crom.

Ulster South

The south of Ulster's four counties, though not as dramatic as those of the north, have a tranquil rural charm that repays closer inspection. This is a country of quiet back roads, imposing lakes and rivers, forests, and gentle mountains.

Cavan's boast of a lake for every day of the year may be a little exaggerated, but its labyrinthine network of lakes and rivers provides a unique setting for gentle hills and small islands. Armagh and Tyrone border onto Lough Neagh, the largest lake in the United Kingdom, while the majestic River Erne flows gently through Fermanagh forming Upper and Lower Lough

Erne, whose many inlets and islands provide a welcome sanctuary for a great variety of birds. The south of Ulster also has its share of historic sights. Monaghan's Bronze Age settlements and pre-historic remains, Fermanagh's island monasteries and *Eamhain Macha* (Navan Fort), the ceremonial capital of the ancient kingdom of Ulster, are significant parts of Ireland's heritage.

The understated and easy-going atmosphere of the south of Ulster is perfectly captured in the Georgian elegance of Armagh City, home to the remains of the High King of Ireland Brian Boru who, in 1014, finally defeated the Viking invaders at the bloody Battle of Clontarf.

Ballykeel Dolmen

ARMAGH

Right. Standing alone by the roadside is the Ballykeel Dolmen, known by locals as the Hag's Chair. Ballykeel Dolmen is a megalith, a Neolithic tomb built with large stones and originally enclosed in a mound of earth. There are four types of megalith, and Ballykeel is an outstanding example of a portal tomb, comprising three large upright stones supporting a capstone. Two larger stones form the entrance to the tomb while a third, smaller one, balances the sloping 'roof' stone.

St Patrick's Cathedral

ARMAGH CITY, ARMAGH

Next page. There are two cathedrals in Armagh City, the place where St Patrick, the first bishop of Armagh, built Ireland's first cathedral in AD 445. St Patrick's Church of Ireland Cathedral is built on the site of St Patrick's original church, and is a much restored and revised medieval structure. St Patrick's Catholic Cathedral, pictured here, dates from the middle of the nineteenth century and has been described as a triumph of the neo-Gothic style, with its twin towers and soaring mosaic-clad interior.

Beaghmore Stone Circles
NEAR COOKSTOWN, TYRONE

Right. Situated in a remote corner of County Tyrone, the Beaghmore Stone Circles are a truly remarkable collection of standing stones. Although the individual stones are not especially large, their number and complexity make this an important Bronze Age site. The site comprises seven circles, ten stone rows and a number of burial mounds. Some of the stone formations were used for astronomical observations and others for ceremonial purposes. Even on a bright summer's day, a tangible air of mystery permeates this ancient monument.

Ulster History Park
NEAR OMAGH, TYRONE

Next page. In 1985, work began on the site of the Ulster History Park and five years later the 14 hectare (35 acre) site was officially opened. Set in the foothills of the beautiful Sperrin Mountains, the Park gives an impression of life in Ulster from the earliest Stone Age settlements onwards. By meticulously following original building methods and avoiding the worst excesses of modern theme park attractions, the History Park gives an authentic introduction to the rich social history of the region.

Sperrin Mountains

TYRONE

Right. Although not the most immediately dramatic of mountain ranges, the Sperrins are a much-loved, if sparsely populated, region. Wild, and with a desolate beauty all of their own, they are an unforgettable sight in spring and summer when the undulating hills are a mass of vivid yellow gorse. Although few people live in the Sperrins, the area is alive with all kinds of wildlife, including buzzards and hawks that circle silently in wait for unsuspecting prey.

Enniskillen Castle

FERMANAGH

Next page. Strikingly floodlit, the vast Portland stone flank and Watergate tower of Enniskillen Castle are reflected in the still waters of the River Erne. The castle was originally built in the fifteenth century by the Maguire clan but was leased to Sir William Cole, an Englishman, during the Plantations of the seventeenth century. A series of repairs, refurbishments and additions over the years, reflecting its strategic importance to the English Crown, led to it becoming a barracks for the Royal Inniskilling Fusiliers.

The province of Connacht contains some of Ireland's most wonderful treasures. It also bears the marks of the suffering of its people, especially during the two great Irish famines of the eighteenth and nineteenth centuries.

There is a remote starkness to much of the landscape here that sits well with the traditional way of life of its Irish-speaking *Gaeltacht* areas. From the fine mountains, lakes and beaches of Leitrim and Sligo that inspired Ireland's greatest poet, W. B. Yeats, to the wild and breathtaking landscapes of Mayo and Achill Island, the north of Connacht transports us back

to an earlier Ireland. Much of the area is relatively unspoiled and retains the spirit of Gaelic Ireland perhaps better than anywhere else in the country. It is typical of the pace of life in Connacht that the first traffic lights in County Leitrim were not installed until 2003.

The influence of the Catholic Church can be felt especially strongly here. Every year, thousands of pilgrims follow in the footsteps of St Patrick climbing the holy mountain of Croagh Patrick, often barefoot. Further inland, the apparition of the Virgin Mary in 1879 has led to the small town of Knock becoming an internationally important Catholic shrine.

Monastic Ruins
INISHMURRAY ISLAND, SLIGO

Right. North along the coast past Sligo Bay lies the uninhabited island of Inishmurray, 8 km (5 miles) off the mainland and fully exposed to the might of the Atlantic. In spite of its inhospitable location the island managed to support a small community of farmers and fishermen until 1948, when the end of the ferry service and closing of the island school forced the last inhabitants to leave for the mainland. Little remains today but the extensive ruins of the sixth century abbey of Saint Molaise.

Classiebawn Castle
MULLAGHMORE, SLIGO

Next page. The building of Classiebawn Castle, high on Mullaghmore Head, was begun by Lord Palmerston, then Prime Minister of England, and completed by his son in 1874. The construction was a major undertaking, as the castle was built entirely of Donegal stone brought by sea to the site. Palmerston also had a harbour created below the house, and it was from here, in 1979, that Lord Mountbatten tragically sailed to his death on board his yacht Shadow V, blown up by the IRA.

Ben Bulben
SLIGO

Right. The flat-topped profile of 'bare Ben Bulben' rises spectacularly from Sligo's coastal plain to its 520 m (1,715 ft) summit overlooking Donegal Bay. This magical limestone massif, seen here from the Donegal side, changes shape dramatically as you round it. Irish mythology tells how Fionn MacCul (Finn MacCool), after searching for seven years, found his son Oisin wandering naked on the mountainside. In the graveyard of Drumcliff's somewhat austere church, Ireland's great poet William Butler Yeats lies buried.

River Garavogue
SLIGO CITY, SLIGO

Next page. Situated at the mouth of the River Garavogue on the narrow strip of land that divides Lough Gill from the sea, Sligo rose to prominence as a port under the Normans. Apart from the thirteenth-century abbey, little of the Norman period remains and most of the modern city was constructed during the nineteenth century. Forming the commercial centre of northwest Ireland with a population of 25,000, Sligo is a bustling, unpretentious place that still manages to retain the relaxed atmosphere so typical of the northwest.

Markree Castle

COLLOONEY, SLIGO

Right. The Cooper family, who currently own Markree Castle, were originally gifted the estate by Oliver Cromwell in lieu of wages owed to Edward Cooper, a young officer in Cromwell's invading English army. Edward married the widow of the leader of the defeated O'Brien clan and settled down to life in County Sligo. Today Charles Cooper, a direct descendent of Edward's third son, owns the castle, which he has run as a hotel since 1989.

Parkes Castle

LOUGH GILL, LEITRIM

Next page. Parkes Castle's idyllic location on the banks of Lough Gill overlooks the lake isle of Innisfree, immortalized by W. B. Yeats' poem of the same name. This attractive Plantation castle was built in the early seventeenth century by Robert Parker on the site of an earlier fortress, which he demolished to provide the stones for the new building. The castle has recently been extensively restored and today looks much as it did when Parker took up residence in 1610.

Glencar Waterfall

LEITRIM

Right. Although Glencar is not the most spectacular of waterfalls, there is something enchanting about the way the water cascades into the lake. Like so many of County Sligo and County Leitrim's beauty spots, Glencar Waterfall, just a short distance south of Manorhamilton, was the inspiration for one of W. B. Yeats' poems, 'The Stolen Child'. Like much of Yeats' work, it expresses nostalgia for what he considered the more romantic, innocent Ireland of the past.

Connacht South

Galway and Roscommon are a good example of the abrupt contrast between the landscapes around the coasts and those of the inland areas of Ireland.

West Galway and the Aran Islands, with their gaily-painted cottages, are some of Ireland's most austerely beautiful areas. The influence of the country's past and its proud Gaelic heritage are apparent everywhere in this sparsely populated area. Travel inland through the Connemara Mountains from the ragged coast where they rise dramatically from the sea, to the shores of Lough Conn and Lough Corrib, and you find yourself in a land far removed from the turmoil of the twenty-first century.

By contrast, Galway City is one of the fastest-growing metropolitan areas in Europe. It maintains its position at the heart of Gaelic culture, while vigorously pursuing a policy of expansion. Galway is reaching out to be recognized as a modern European city of culture, and is already famous for its international arts festivals and the quality of its robust hospitality.

County Galway, east of Lough Corrib and Roscommon, is far more pastoral. This lowland region of Connacht is an area of rich grazing land, extensive peat bogs and fertile farmland.

Boyle Abbey

ROSCOMMON

Right. The Cistercian order of monks founded Boyle Abbey in 1161 as a sister abbey for Mellifont, their first abbey in Ireland, which they established twenty years earlier. In common with all Cistercian abbeys, Boyle was constructed according to the plan of St Gall and consists of a group of structures that form a square arranged around a central lawned area. The abbey was converted into a fortified castle by Cromwell's English forces in 1659, but survives today remarkably intact.

Castle Island

LOUGH KEY FOREST PARK, BOYLE, ROSCOMMON

Next page. Lough Key, often described as Ireland's loveliest stretch of inland water, is a five km- (three mile-) wide circular lake in the heart of the Lough Key Forest Park. Castle Island is one of the lake's 33 islands and the site of a ruined nineteenth century castle. The poet Yeats was so impressed, both with the castle and the island, that he planned to make it a centre for the study and contemplation of mystical Ireland.

Lily Pool and Temple
STROKESTOWN PARK, ROSCOMMON

Right. Strokestown Park is a splendid eighteenth-century Palladian mansion famous for its collection of original furnishings. In 1997, after a ten-year restoration programme, Strokestown's 2.5-hectare (six-acre) walled gardens were opened to the public for the first time. Among the many original features that have been faithfully restored are this magnificent lily pond and ornamental temple. The gardens appear in the Guinness Book of Records for possessing the longest herbaceous border in the whole of the British Isles.

Kylemore
GALWAY

Next page. Mitchell Henry, a Manchester millionaire, built Kylemore Abbey, a nineteenth-century Gothic Revivalist fantasy on the shores of Fannon Pool, as a gift for his wife after they honeymooned in the area. When his wife and daughter tragically died he sold the property, and in 1916 Kylemore became the Irish home of the Order of Benedictine Nuns, driven from their abbey in Ypres, France, by the bombs of the First World War. Today the nuns run a thriving girls' school at Kylemore.

Bunowen Bay and Twelve Pins
CONNEMARA, GALWAY

Right. The twelve imposing summits of the Twelve Pins form an impressive backdrop for the pier harbour at Bunowen Bay. Wherever you are in Connemara, the Twelve Pins, or Bens as they are known locally, dominate the view. Benbaun is the highest peak, rising to 729 m (2,400 ft) while the lowest, Bengoora, also called Diamond Hill, climbs to 400 m (1,329 ft). Part of the Maumturk Mountains, this distinctive range of hills provides excellent hill-walking country with memorable views.

Derryclare Lough
CONNEMARA, GALWAY

Next page. The Maumturks, shrouded in cloud, stand between the placid waters of Derryclare Lough and the sea. This almost mystical scene can be little changed from the times of the Celts who first settled on the west coast of Ireland more than 2,500 years ago. On the western shores of the lough there is a nature reserve of ancient oak woodland, funded by the Irish American Cultural Foundation in appreciation of the contribution emigrants from Galway have made to the life of Boston.

Dogs Bay
NEAR ROUNDSTONE, CONNEMARA, GALWAY

Right. Relaxing in Dogs Bay on a warm sunny day you could almost imagine yourself on a Caribbean island. This beautiful sheltered inlet with its crescent-shaped shoreline is just two miles from Roundstone Harbour, one of Connemara's oldest resorts, on the south coast of Galway Bay. The pure white sand of Dogs Bay is formed exclusively of shells, and the temperate currents of the Gulf Stream warm its clear, aquamarine water.

Galway City
GALWAY

Next page. Walking through its welcoming streets and pleasant squares, you might find it hard to believe that Galway City at the mouth of Lough Corrib is one of the fastest growing urban areas in the European Union. Of all Ireland's cities, Galway is the one that best combines the modern Ireland of the Celtic Tiger with the easy-going vibrancy and cultural richness that is its Gaelic heritage. The gentle harbour with its fishing boats moored to the stone walls give little hint of the activity beyond.

Dunguaire Castle
KINVARA, GALWAY

Right. Close to the port at Kinvara, Dunguaire Castle is a small, sixteenth-century fortress marvellously situated on a rocky promontory overlooking the majestic sweep of Galway Bay. In the early twentieth century the castle, built in 1520, became the venue for the meeting of a group of distinguished literary revivalists including W. B. Yeats, his patron Lady Gregory, and the playwrights George Bernard Shaw and J. M. Synge. Today it plays host to somewhat more prosaic twice-nightly medieval banquets.

Dun Aengus Fort, Inishmore
ARAN ISLANDS, GALWAY

Next page. Dun Aengus is an awesome place, from its heart-stopping setting atop a cliff 100 m (330 ft) high to its four concentric rings of drystone wall. These are up to 4 m (13 ft) thick in places, which, along with the jagged protrusions seen here in the foreground, seems to confirm the traditional view that Dun Aengus was a fort. Modern archeologists are not so sure, though: they suspect that it was built in the Bronze Age – in 1000 BC, or even earlier – as a ritual site for religious ceremonies of some sort.

Leinster North

The landlocked counties of Longford, Westmeath and Kildare, and the east coast counties of Louth, Dublin, Meath and Offaly make up what is generally referred to as the Midlands or, more exactly, the Central Lowlands.

Though the region tends to be ignored in favour of its more dramatic and immediately alluring neighbours, Leinster contains some of Ireland's most sacred and culturally important sites. Indeed, these counties are accurately described as the cradle of Irish civilization. As well as lush pastures, rolling hills, lakes and raised peat-land bogs, the Central Lowlands are home to the Republic's capital city Dublin, as well as

Tara, the spiritual centre of ancient Ireland and seat of the High Kings of Ireland until the eleventh century.

Monuments of the stature of the Neolithic passage graves of Newgrange dating from 3,000 BC, eleventh-century Mellifont Abbey and the vast Norman fortress at Trim in County Meath, all tell a tale of Ireland just as impressive as the mighty cliffs of Donegal or the otherworldly landscape of County Clare's Burren. The north of Leinster can also offer fine beaches, elegant seaside resorts, and some of the finest horse racing to be found anywhere in the world.

River Shannon

ATHLONE TOWN, WESTMEATH

Right. The Shannon rises in County Fermanagh, flowing through no less than 11 of Ireland's 32 counties on its way to the sea. By the time the river reaches Athlone, roughly mid-way on its journey, it has formed several major loughs. The bustling town of Athlone owes its existence to a natural fording point in the river. Here the twin towers of the church of St Peter and St Paul are strikingly reflected in the Shannon's calm waters.

Traditional Pub

MOATE, WESTMEATH

Next page. On the main street of the small village of Moate in Westmeath, Egan's Bar provides a bold splash of colour. Minimal in style, not even displaying the ubiquitous Guinness adverts, the Gaelic-style name ranges boldly across the length of the frontage. The deep red paintwork and the two large plain windows combine to produce an effect that is modern while retaining the feel of a bygone era. Egan's bar has that easy, natural elegance that even professional designers struggle to achieve.

Burial Chamber and Standing Stone
NEWGRANGE, MEATH

Right. A summer sun shines over the mysterious burial chamber and standing stone at Newgrange. Celtic tradition suggests that this is the burial place of the legendary kings of Tara, but in fact the chamber predates them by thousands of years. When the tomb was excavated, archaeologists discovered that the light of the winter solstice sun entered the tomb, illuminating the burial chamber. Remarkably, the burial chamber at Newgrange, in this quiet corner of County Meath, is the world's oldest solar observatory.

Trim Castle
TRIM, MEATH

Next page. Trim, now a lively market town in the centre of historic County Meath, was once intended to be Ireland's capital. The most obvious sign of its former glory is the considerable size of Trim Castle, the largest Anglo-Norman castle in Ireland. The massive twenty-sided cruciform tower that forms the three-storied keep was built in around 1200 by Hugh de Lacy, the first Norman baron of Meath. The castle was extensively restored in 2000 as part of Ireland's Millennium Project.

Birr Castle
OFFALY

Right. In the mid-nineteenth century, the 3rd Earl of Ross, whose family had lived in Birr Castle since its construction in 1620, possessed what was then the largest astronomical telescope in the world, the 'Leviathan'. Birr is equally famous for the splendour of its grounds, which extend to over 60 hectares (150 acres) of parkland and gardens, first laid out in the eighteenth century. Succeeding Earls of Ross have added to the exotic plants and trees on display, often sponsoring foreign expeditions to gather more.

The Abbey at Clonmacnoise
OFFALY

Next page. St Ciaran originally founded the first church on the ancient monastic site at Clonmacnoise in AD 545. Strategically located on the banks of the Shannon at the intersection of a number of important medieval roads, the site supported a religious community that thrived throughout the Middle Ages. Among the remains that survive today are a fifteenth-century cathedral, a fine round tower, many small churches and an important collection of ancient tombstones and thousand-year-old High Crosses.

Sculpture of Jim Larkin and the Spire
O'CONNELL STREET, DUBLIN

Right. In the centre of O'Connell Street, Dublin's principle thoroughfare, stand monuments to Ireland's past and its future. In the foreground, the oversized hands of Big Jim Larkin, the founder of the Irish Transport and General Workers Union in 1909, exhort the workers to rise up against injustice. Behind Jim rises the 120 m (390 ft) high Dublin Spire, the city's tallest structure by some measure. This futuristic stainless steel creation was the winner of a millennium competition to replace the little-loved Nelson's Column, blown up in 1966.

River Liffey
DUBLIN

Next page. The River Liffey flows through the heart of Dublin and lends much to the character of this elegant Georgian city. The Vikings established the original settlement in the eighth century, naming it from the Irish words *dubh* ('black'), and *linn* ('pool'). It is thought this referred to a black pool in a tributary of the Liffey, which has long since been drained and built over. In the middle ground is Ha'penny Bridge, reflected in the Liffey in the evening light.

O'Connell Street
DUBLIN

Right. Daniel O'Connell, in statue form, looks out from the lower end of the street which bears his name across the bridge that was also named for the 'Liberator'. O'Connell it was who, in the early nineteenth century, won Ireland's Catholics the right to religious freedom and political representation and did much to advance the cause of nationalism in the country. Till 1924, Dublin's main thoroughfare was known as 'Sackville Street', after Lionel Cranfield Sackville, Duke of Dorset, an eighteenth-century Lord Lieutenant, but the newly independent nation wanted to commemorate its hero.

Trinity College
DUBLIN

Next page. Founded by a Royal Charter of Queen Elizabeth I in 1592, Trinity College is one of the world's great seats of learning and, in 1904, it was the first of the ancient universities of the British Isles to admit women. Its manicured lawns and elegant quadrangles have played host to extremely distinguished alumni, including the Nobel Prize-winners Samuel Beckett and Ernest Walton. The 30 m (100 ft) high campanile that confronts visitors as they enter the campus was designed in 1853 by the architect Sir Charles Lanyon.

Dublin Castle
DUBLIN

Right. On 16 January 1922, following the signing of the Anglo-Irish Treaty, the rebel commander Michael Collins arrived in the Great Courtyard, pictured here, to receive the handover of Dublin Castle. So ended seven long centuries when the castle was one of the most prominent symbols of English rule in Ireland. Following Irish independence, the castle was allowed to fall into disrepair, a decaying symbol of a painful past. Now it is fully restored and integrated into Irish life.

The Four Courts
DUBLIN

Next page. There are only three, in fact – the Irish Supreme Court, the High Court and the Central Criminal Court – but the name has endured from the days of English rule. Then these buildings housed the Chancery, the King's Bench, the Exchequer and the Court of Common Claims. Viewing it from a distance, you would never know that this elegant Georgian complex was all but demolished during the Civil War of the 1920s. Up-close, though, bullet-holes may still be seen in the stonework, a reminder of the fighting of that time.

The Dail
GOVERNMENT BUILDINGS, DUBLIN

Right. The Duke of Leinster, who wanted to live in the stateliest mansion in Dublin, originally commissioned Leinster House in 1745. Designed by the German Richard Cassells, it is said to have been a major influence on James Hoban, the Irish architect of the White House in Washington. Since the proclamation of the Irish Free State in 1922, Leinster House has been the seat of the two chambers of the Irish Parliament, Dáil Éireann (the House of Representatives) and Seanad Éireann (the Senate).

Custom House
RIVER LIFFEY, DUBLIN

Next page. Of the many notable buildings that the English architect James Gandon designed for Dublin, his crowning achievement was the majestic Custom House on the north bank of the Liffey. Ironically, less than a decade after its completion, the 1800 Act of Union made the building's principal function as the centre for Ireland's customs and excise business redundant. Having fallen into disrepair, and set on fire by Sinn Féin supporters in 1921, it was restored to its former glory in 1991.

Ha'penny Bridge
DUBLIN

Right. Ha'penny Bridge, an iconic symbol of Dublin, was originally called Wellington Bridge after the 'Iron Duke'. Today its formal name is the Liffey Bridge, although it is seldom referred to as anything other than Ha'penny Bridge. Opened in 1816, the bridge was designed and built by John Windsor, the ironwork being produced in Shropshire and shipped to Dublin for assembly. When it was opened there was a toll of half a penny to cross it, and its nickname, Ha'penny Bridge, has stuck.

Christ Church Cathedral
DUBLIN

Next page. Dublin has two cathedrals but, unusually for such a Catholic country, both are part of the Protestant Church of Ireland. Richard de Clare, Dublin's Anglo-Norman conqueror, founded Christ Church in 1172. It was built on the site of an earlier Viking church and became a protestant church at the time of the English Reformation. The cathedral was extensively remodelled in the late nineteenth century, and the bridge to Synod Hall, shown here, was built as part of that work.

Leinster South

The south of Leinster is the driest and sunniest corner of Ireland, home to ancient monuments, monasteries, fine houses and magnificent gardens.

The gentle seashores of Wicklow and Wexford reflect their sheltered aspect in much the same way as the wild west coast testifies to the insatiable power of the Atlantic. The southeastern coastline is one of dazzling beaches of silver sand, secluded river estuaries, rocky headlands and quiet coastal villages. Further inland, the wild and threatening beauty of the Wicklow Mountains forms a powerful backdrop for the ancient monastic site of Glendalough, and the formal garden at Powerscourt and Mount Usher. The Wicklow

Mountains, once bandit country and home to successive groups of Irish dissidents, are a pointed reminder of Ireland's turbulent past in this comfortable, conservative region.

Beyond the Wicklow Mountains spread green pastures, wooded valleys and swiftly flowing rivers. There are fine towns and pretty villages here too, none more stylish than the inland city of Kilkenny. Reminders of the suffering caused by the great potato famines temper the south of Leinster's easy-going elegance, however. The 'famine walls' that surround many of the great houses of the area were built simply to provide work for the famine's survivors.

Pleached Lime Alley
HEYWOOD GARDENS, LAOIS

Right. Shakespeare refers to a 'thick pleached allee' in Much Ado About Nothing, and an elegant avenue of pleached lime trees was a typical feature of many formal English gardens from the fourteenth century onwards. Completed in 1912, Heywood Gardens in County Laois was the work of two distinguished English designers: the architect Sir Edwin Lutyens and the landscape gardener Gertrude Jekyll. As well as the formal elements, the gardens include lakes, woodlands and architectural features.

Stradbally
LAOIS

Next page. The gentle landscape of County Laois, with its lush pastures and neatly laid-out fields, is typical of Ireland's central lowlands. The fertile soil of Laois has attracted settlers from the earliest times. Here and in neighbouring Offaly, the British policy of Plantation was used extensively to secure a base around the Pale, the seat of English authority. This verdant countryside is close to the elegant 'estate town' of Abbeyleix, carefully laid out during the Plantations.

St Joseph's Square
MAYNOOTH COLLEGE, KILDARE

Right. When George III signed the authorization for a Catholic seminary at Maynooth, he remarked that it gave him more pain to do so than losing the American colonies. St Patrick's College, seen here from St Joseph's Square, was founded as the National Seminary for Ireland in 1795, allowing Catholic priests to be educated in Ireland for the first time since the early sixteenth century. Parts of the square are the works of Augustus Pugin, better known as one of the two architects of the Palace of Westminster.

River Liffey
WICKLOW

Next page. The Liffey is a wonderfully meandering waterway that seems somehow ideally suited to the Irish temperament. The first sentence of James Joyce's novel *Finnegan's Wake* refers to it as a river that, '…brings us by a commodious viscus of recirculation back to Howth Castle and Environs'. Though it rises only 19 km (12 miles) from Dublin, the river takes more than 120 leisurely km (75 miles) to reach its final destination, passing through three counties, Wicklow, Kildare and Dublin, on its way.

Powerscourt Gardens
WICKLOW

Right. A garden of international importance, Powerscourt stands as testimony to the might and wealth of the eighteenth century Anglo-Irish Protestant Ascendancy. Magnificently located in the shadow of the Great and Little Sugarloaf Mountains, everything at Powerscourt is on a grand scale. The formal gardens, sweeping terraces, ornamental lakes and rambling walks cover an area of over 560 immaculately maintained hectares (1,400 acres). Even the drive leading up to the Palladian House is almost 1.65 km (1 mile) long.

Wicklow Mountains
WICKLOW

Next page. The Wicklow Mountains are close enough to Dublin to be easily visible from there, but it would be difficult to imagine two more contrasting locations. Even the surrounding countryside gives no hint of the wild and desolate scenery of the mountains. In the past, the inaccessibility of the terrain made the Wicklow Mountains bandit country, a lawless area where insurgents could hide out just a stone's throw from the capital. Today they provide excellent hiking and climbing terrain.

Glendalough

WICKLOW

Right. The view of the valley of Glendalough and the eleventh century round tower of St Kevin's monastery are one of County Wicklow's enduring images. The monastic community that St Kevin established in the sixth century survived repeated attacks from the Vikings, flourishing for more than 600 years as a centre of learning renowned throughout Europe. The 34 m (112 ft) high round tower itself has survived virtually intact, only the cap having been restored in the 1870s using the original stones.

Glendalough

WICKLOW MOUNTAINS, WICKLOW

Next page. The name Glendalough means 'Glen of Two Lakes' in Irish, an apt enough description: here we see the 'Upper Lake' in its rugged mountain setting. Today it is deserted but, as recently as the 1950s, there were lead miners living in a little village up here. Leinster is a lovely part of Ireland, but its scenery is unspectacular for the most part: the Wicklow Mountains are the great exception. Lugnaquilla, the range's highest peak, rises to 925 m (3,035 ft): in fine conditions you can see clear across to Wales.

Kilkenny Castle

KILKENNY

Right. The splendid medieval form of Kilkenny Castle rises imposingly above Kilkenny City. There has been a castle on this site since 1172 when Richard de Clare, the notorious Strongbow, built the first one. Constructed in 1213, the stone 'keep-less' castle with its massive drum towers forms the heart of what remains today. Although the castle retains its original medieval appearance, much of the structure was rebuilt in the seventeenth and again in the nineteenth centuries.

River Barrow

AT GRAIGUENAMANAGH, KILKENNY

Next page. As the River Barrow flows through the fertile countryside of County Kilkenny, navigation for the many pleasure-craft that use the river is made possible by an extensive system of locks. The tranquil atmosphere of Clashganny Lock at Graiguenamanagh is perfectly suited to the leisurely progress of the river at this point. Graiguenamanagh is reinventing itself as the 'Town of Books', and for one week every September it plays host to booksellers, buyers and writers from all over Ireland and increasingly from overseas.

Kilmore Quay
WEXFORD

Right. Kilmore Quay is a delightfully unspoilt little village of thatched cottages with whitewashed walls gathered around a stonewall harbour. Moored in the harbour, the perfectly preserved 1923 lightship *The Guillemot* is home to the Kilmore Maritime Museum and, from the quay, boat trips leave for the nearby Saltee Islands, where there are puffins, gannets and large colonies of cormorants. The area is noted for the quality of the lobster and deep-sea fishing, and the village holds a hugely popular Sea Festival in July.

Booley Bay
HOOK PENINSULA, WEXFORD

Next page. On the tapering headland of the Hook Peninsula, the sun sets dramatically on the ebbing tide at Booley Bay. Booley shelters in the estuary of the River Barrow, an area of 'lost' villages overcome by tidal silting and floodwaters driven by tides and strong winds running up the coast. Just inland from the shifting sands of the bay is Duncannon, where in 1690 James II finally fled Ireland after his disastrous defeat at the Battle of the Boyne.

Hook Head

WEXFORD

Right. Lighthouses are by their nature remarkable buildings, and few are more astounding than the lighthouse at Hook Head. There may have been a lighthouse on this site earlier, but we know for sure that in 1172 the Norman Raymond le Gros built the existing structure with its 4 m (13 ft) thick walls. Originally manned by monks, the lighthouse's peat-fire beacon was guiding sailors into the safety of the Waterford Estuary more than six centuries before the pioneering eighteenth-century British lighthouses of James Smeaton.

Munster North

Even in a country so blessed with stunning scenery, Munster is special. The counties of the north of Munster are united by Ireland's longest river, the majestic Shannon, which flows through all three of them on the final stages of its journey to the Atlantic. However, the coastal scenery and relative emptiness of County Clare contrast with the more populous and fertile counties of Limerick and Tipperary.

Among its many treasures, County Clare has two defining geological features. In the north of the county lies the austere landscape of the Burren. This vast desolate limestone plateau

shows little sign of life other than the truly remarkable diversity of Alpine and Mediterranean flowers and plants that reappear every summer. Further south, facing out to the Aran Islands and the ocean's gales are the Cliffs of Moher. Their vertiginous sheer rock faces, home to legions of seabirds, form one of the most dramatic outlooks of Ireland's breathtaking west coast.

Limerick and Tipperary cannot compete with the drama of the Clare coast, but both counties have more than their share of pleasant towns, country estates, ruined castles, abbeys and ancient monuments, all set in gentle, rolling landscapes.

Poulnabrone Dolmen
THE BURREN, CLARE

Right. In the heart of the stark landscape of the Burren stands the magnificent Poulnabrone dolmen. Poulnabrone, a wedge tomb, is the finest of over 70 ancient burial sites to be found in the Burren's limestone uplands and consists of four upright stones supporting a thin capstone. When the tomb was excavated in the 1960s, the remains of 20 adults, five children and a newborn baby were uncovered. Subsequent carbon dating calculated the burials took place between 3800 and 3200 BC.

Cliffs of Moher
CLARE

Next page. Although not as high as the cliffs at Slieve League in County Donegal, the Cliffs of Moher are every bit as dramatic. Rising vertically to a height of 200 m (650 ft) out of the crashing waves of the Atlantic, their sheer rock faces extend for over eight km (five miles) along the coast of County Clare. In any light, the contrasting layers of sandstone and shale of which the cliffs are composed make a breathtaking sight as the sun sets into the ocean.

Adare

LIMERICK

Right. Situated on the Maigue, a tributary of the Shannon, Adare takes it name from the Gaelic *Ath Dara*, the 'ford of the oak'. The old town of Adare, in the shadow of Desmond Castle, was destroyed during the wars of the sixteenth century. The present village, with its irresistibly picturesque thatched and whitewashed cottages, dates back to the nineteenth century when the Earl of Dunraven laid out the streets and built the dwellings according to his own design.

Rock of Cashel

TIPPERARY

Next page. Rising up on a limestone outcrop beside the Dublin to Cork road is the great stone fort of Cashel, with its 28 m (93 ft) high round tower scanning the horizon for potential attacks. From the fourth century Cashel was the seat of the Kings of Munster and Brian Boru, who was crowned here in 977. In 1100 Cashel was handed over to the church and a religious community flourished here until 1647 when Cromwell's army lay siege to it, finally massacring its 3,000 inhabitants.

Cahir Castle
TIPPERARY

Right. The busy market town of Cahir on the River Suir was once an important garrison town. Its castle, built on a rocky island in the middle of the river, is one of the most redoubtable of Ireland's many well-fortified bastions. Built in the thirteenth century, the castle was the domain of the powerful Anglo-Norman Butler family from 1375 until 1964. The Butlers maintained their castle well, renovating and extending it periodically through the centuries so that today it remains remarkably well preserved.

The Swiss Cottage
NEAR CAHIR, TIPPERARY

Next page. The enchanting Swiss Cottage provides a wonderful antidote to formidable Cahir Castle. In 1810 the Butlers commissioned John Nash, the English Regency architect, to produce a rustic folly in the grounds of their castle. Nash's design for Swiss Cottage, a cottage orné, fulfils all the elaborate conditions of that genre, where all the features of the design are drawn from nature and nothing matches. Every window, door, archway, roofline and eve of the cottage is of differing dimensions and design.

Holy Cross Abbey

NEAR THURLES, TIPPERARY

Right. The Abbey of Holy Cross was founded by Benedictines in 1169 and taken over by the Cistercians a decade later. Most of the carefully restored structures on this important religious site date from the fifteenth century, when the abbey came under the protection of the fourth Earl of Ormonde, James Butler. The 1896 Irish Church Act transferred the abbey into the care of the state, but in 1969, by special act of parliament, Holy Cross's status as a place of worship was restored.

Munster South

The three counties that form the south of Munster track the coastline's transformation from the storm-tossed ruggedness of the west coast to the relative tranquillity and sweeping bays of the south and southeast.

Wild and mountainous County Kerry, still referred to as 'the Kingdom' because of its history of fierce independence from central government, has some of Ireland's finest scenery, its greatest pre-historic and early Christian monuments and some of its best beaches. Killarney National Park, with its romantic lakes and mountains, has been a fashionable tourist destination since Victorian times, and the Dingle Peninsula's combination of

enchanting scenery and important historic sites makes it an outstanding area of international renown. County Cork's slightly more sheltered southerly aspect has produced a shoreline of impressive bays and magnificent headlands, gentle harbours and long, golden strands. Inland, Cork is a county of rich farmland and pleasant rural backwaters. It is also home to Blarney Castle, resting place of the Blarney Stone, that legendary source of the nation's eloquence. Waterford City, founded by Vikings in the ninth century, is Ireland's oldest city, and a thriving European port. The countryside of County Waterford, though less dramatic than its two larger neighbours, is no less beautiful.

Annascaul

THE DINGLE PENINSULA, KERRY

Right. The village of Annascaul is situated in the southern foothills of the Slieve Mish Mountains that form the backbone of the Dingle Peninsula. The local beach, Inch Strand, was the location for David Lean's film Ryan's Daughter. Annascaul's own claim to fame is Dan Foley's pub and more particularly its brilliantly colourful frontage, which the late, and somewhat eccentric, Dan painted himself some years ago. Foley's is said to be the most photographed pub in Ireland.

Slea Head

THE DINGLE PENINSULA, KERRY

Next page. Looking west from Slea Head, across Coumeenoole Bay, lies Dunmore Head, mainland Ireland's most westerly point. Beyond the Head, across Blasket Sound, are the Blasket Islands, uninhabited since 1953, but once the home of a close-knit community of farmers and fishermen who eked out a living on this inhospitable but beautiful spot 3.2 km (two miles) off the coast. There are two internationally celebrated accounts of life on the Blasket Islands written by past inhabitants: Maurice O'Sullivan's *Twenty Years A-Growing*, and *Peig* by Peig Sayer.

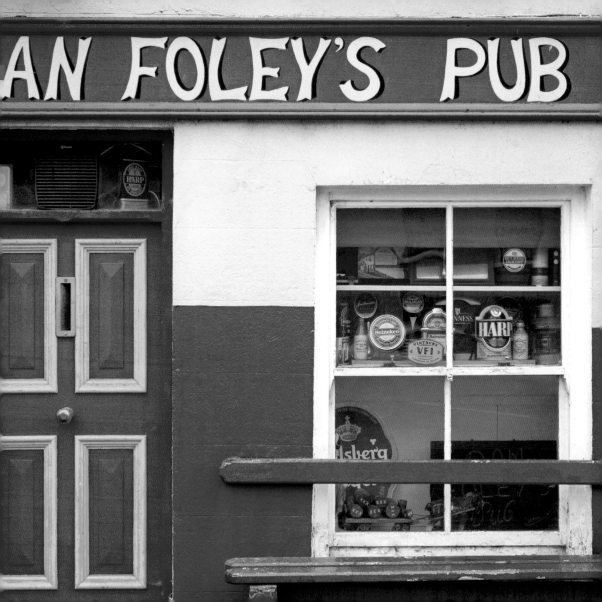

Lough Currane
WATERVILLE, KERRY

Right. A narrow isthmus is all that divides Lough Currane from the sea in Ballinskelligs Bay. This tranquil spot on the Ring of Kerry, in the foothills of the Coomcalee Mountains, has a number of interesting historic ruins including the sixth-century Oratory of St Finan, a twelfth century Hiberno-Romanesque church, and a partially submerged castle. What brings most people to Lough Currane is its fish, however, and the lough is acknowledged as one of the greatest game-fishing locations in Europe.

Derrynane Bay
DEENISH & SCARIFF ISLANDS, KERRY

Next page. As well as having some of the most spectacular scenery in the world, Kerry's west-facing coast enjoys some wonderfully memorable sunsets. Here, looking west from Lamb's Head on the southern tip of Derrynane Bay, the sun sets over the small islands of Deenish and Scariff. The bay, with its well-hidden natural harbour, was a spot much favoured by smugglers. Daniel O'Connell, the 'Liberator', who won the vote for Irish Catholics in the nineteenth century, lived at nearby Derrynane House.

Sneem Sculpture Park
KERRY

Right. Beside the swirling waters of the River Sneem stands a cluster of pyramid-like structures in local stone, some of them incorporating brightly coloured sections of stained glass. Taken as a whole, they form a collective sculpture to which their creator, Kerry artist James Scanlon, has given the name 'The Way the Fairies Went'. This is just the centrepiece of a remarkable assemblage of sculptures, including works by internationally acclaimed artists like Tamara Rikman and Vivienne Roche – and even a stone panda, donated by the People's Republic of China.

Sneem
RING OF KERRY, KERRY

Next page. Midway between Kenmare and Waterville, Sneem is a pleasant riverside town at the head of the Sneem, a tributary of the Kenmare. Like many of the towns and villages on the Ring of Kerry, Sneem has re-invented itself as a tourist destination, naming itself the 'Knot in the Ring', *sneem* being the Gaelic for 'knot'. Its principal hotel, the Parknasilla, lays claim to the unusual distinction of having hosted George Bernard Shaw, President De Gaulle of France and the Queen of the Netherlands.

Waterville
RING OF KERRY, KERRY

Right. Situated on the narrow isthmus between Ballinskelligs Bay and Lough Currane, Waterville is one of the more sophisticated resorts on the Kerry coast. Its stony beach and wild views of the ocean made it popular with Victorians and Edwardians wanting to get away from the excesses of the more popular resorts further around the coast. Today it maintains its rather limpid air of nineteenth century elegance and is famous for having been Charlie Chaplin's regular choice for family holidays.

Torc Waterfall
RING OF KERRY, KERRY

Next page. A much-photographed feature and popular stopping point on the Ring of Kerry is the Torc Waterfall that tumbles into Muckross Lake, one of the three lakes in the Killarney National Park. The 18 m (60 ft) high waterfall marks the mouth of the Owengariff River as it ends its journey from the Torc Mountains through the woods of Friar's Glen. A pretty path winds up to a viewing platform at the top of the falls from where there are splendid views of the mountains.

Garinish Island

CORK

Right. The southwest corner of Ireland, particularly west Cork, is blessed with the warming currents of the Gulf Stream, resulting in relatively mild springs and autumns. The 15 hectare (38 acre) island garden of Garnish, situated in the sheltered waters of the Glengarriff Estuary in Bantry Bay, takes full advantage of the temperate climate. Known to horticulturists worldwide, this remarkable collection of exotic plants and shrubs was first laid out in 1910 by the owner Annan Bryce and the architect and garden designer Harold Peto.

Allihies

BEARA PENINSULA, CORK

Next page.. Lying between the southern shore of the Kenmare River and Bantry Bay, the Beara Peninsula marks the start of the transition from wild County Kerry to the increasingly more gentle coastal landscapes of County Cork. The peninsula itself is dominated by the Slieve Miskish and Caha Mountains that run down its spine. Allihies on the more exposed northern coast in Ballydonegan Bay is famous for the ruined Berehaven copper mine, which had an operational depth of over 450 m (1,485 ft).

Red Strand and Galley Head
CORK

Right. The sandy beaches of West Cork's southern coast are famous for their safe bathing and the natural beauty of their locations. Red Strand is a glorious stretch of golden sand that forms a bay between the two headlands of Galley Head and Dunowen Head. The beach itself is not actually red, its name coming from the colour of the cliffs that shelter it. The area around is particularly noted for its birdlife, and the presence of the wrecks of numerous ships, popular with divers.

Blarney Castle
CORK

Next page. Blarney Castle, built in 1446 by Dermot McCarthy, King of Munster, is one of Ireland's oldest and most historic fortresses. The castle was the third to be built on the site by the McCarthys, whose stronghold it remained until Cromwell finally took it in the seventeenth century. Impressive as the castle is, it is the presence of the Blarney Stone, now rather prosaically referred to as the Stone of Eloquence, that makes Blarney Castle so internationally famous.

Cobh Cathedral
CORK

Right. Known by the Anglo-Irish name of Queenstown for many years, Cobh reverted to its Irish name in 1922 with the founding of the Irish Free State. A pleasant town situated on Great Island in Cork's extensive harbour, Cobh was the embarkation point for hundreds of thousands of Irish men and women forced to leave their homeland by famine and persecution. Cobh's Catholic Cathedral, designed by the celebrated English architects Pugin and Ashlin, is a fine example of the neo-Gothic style.

Lismore Castle
WATERFORD

Next page. Lismore has been the home of the Dukes of Devonshire since the marriage of the fourth Duke to Lady Charlotte Boyle (a descendant of Robert Boyle, the father of modern chemistry) in 1753. It is a marvellously preserved structure, parts of which date back to the thirteenth century. The castle has had more than its share of illustrious residents, having been the property of Sir Walter Raleigh, the Boyle family and the home for the first part of his life of Joseph Paxton, designer of the Crystal Palace in London.

Burial Site of Samuel Grubb

KNOCKMEALDOWN MOUNTAINS, WATERFORD

Right. The 18-km (11-mile) long road that winds dramatically through the Knockmealdown Mountains, from Clogheen to Lismore in County Waterford, is one of Ireland's great scenic drives. Known as the 'Vee', the road reaches its high point at the Tipperary–Waterford border and it is here that Samuel Grubb, a former High Sheriff of Tipperary, is buried. Such was his love of the countryside that he insisted on being buried upright on the slopes of Sugar Loaf Hill, overlooking the Golden Vale and the lush plains of Tipperary.

Dungarvan

NEAR WATERFORD, WATERFORD

Next page. Dungarvan, a charming seaside town, is part of what now describes itself as the Irish Riviera, an area of the south coast that spreads east from Cobh in County Cork to Dungarvan itself, and includes the resorts of Ballycotton, Youghal and Ardmore. The town is grandly positioned beneath the Drum Hills at the head of the bay that forms Dungavan Harbour. It combines the roles of market town, port and tourist resort with an easy-going energy.

Spraoi Festival

WATERFORD CITY, WATERFORD

Right. Every August Bank Holiday the streets of Waterford's city centre are taken over by the Spraoi Festival. *Spraoi* is a Gaelic word meaning celebration or party, and since 1993, when the festival first started as a one-day event, it has gone from strength to strength. Today this unique street party lasts the whole weekend, transforming Waterford's streets and quays into a giant stage for acts from all over the world and attracting audiences in excess of 80,000.

Acknowledgements

Biographies

Kevin Eyres (text) qualified as an arts teacher at the University of East Anglia. He has a master's degree in European cultural policy. As well as writing extensively on modern art and media-related topics, Kevin has written on various aspects of Irish cultural life and the great Irish literary figures of the nineteenth and twentieth centuries. One of his earliest memories is riding to the local creamery on a horse and cart to deliver milk from his grandparents' farm on the Kerry/Limerick borders.

Michael Kerrigan (text) lives in Edinburgh, where he writes regularly for the *Scotsman* newspaper. He is a book reviewer for *The Times Literary Supplement* and the *Guardian*, London. As an author, he has published extensively on both British and world history and prehistory. He has been a contributor to Flame Tree's *World History* and *Irish History* as well as to *The Times Encyclopaedia of World Religion* (2001). His contributions to this book can be found on the following pages: 20(t), 20(b), 52(b), 128(b), 148(t), 156(b), 180(b), 228(t).

Picture Credits

Courtesy of Superstock (www.superstock.com) and the following: LOOK–foto 21; Martin Siepmann/imageBROKER 22–23; Nomad 25; The Irish Image Collection 26–27, 34–35, 38–39, 45, 58–59, 61, 62–63, 69, 75, 76–77, 79, 80–81, 84–85, 87, 88–89, 95, 99, 103, 104–105, 117, 122–123, 138–139, 141, 145, 173, 174, 177, 204–205, 222–223, 225, 229, 233, 249; Martin Siepmann/imageBROKER 57; imageBROKER 29, 107; Tibor Bognár/age fotostock 53; BlueGreen Pictures 64; Chris Hill/National Geographic 96–97; Peter Zoeller/Design Pics 113; Robert Harding Picture Library 125, 129, 221; Steve Vidler 137; F1 ONLINE 142–143, 146–47; Travel Library Limited 157; Chris Hill/National Geographic 161; Brian Jannsen/age fotostock 166–67; riganmc 178–79; George Munday/age fotostock 185, 190–91, 193, 197, 253; Andrew Michael/age fotostock 207; Ivan Vdovin/age fotostock 208–209; Peter Zoeller/Design Pics 212–13; Peter Barritt 234–235; Nikhilesh Haval/age fotostock 245.

Courtesy of Shutterstock (www.shutterstock.com) and the following: Daz Brown Photography 42–43; Kanuman 46–47; Aitormmfoto 49, 149; MMacKillop 50–51; PHB.cz (Richard Semik) 54–55; Ryan Simpson 66–67; Jane McIlroy 121; EcoPrint 118–119; Gabriela Insuratelu 126–127; Pavel L Photo and Video 150–51; David Soanes 154–55; Artur Bogacki 158–59; matthi 162–163; walshphotos 237, 242–243, 250–251; PHB.cz (Richard Semik) 238–39; Captblack 76, 241.

Courtesy of Getty (www.gettyimages.co.uk) and the following: Shaun Egan 30–31; 33 Charles Bowman; Joe Daniel Price 37; www.deirdregregg.com 41; Chris Hill 75, 181; Gareth McCormac 83; IIC/Axiom 100–101, 114–115, 189, 226–27; Robin Bush 130–131, 246–247; Photodisc 153, 165; Joe Cornish 182–83; Maciej Frolow 186–87; Trish Punch 194–95; Robert Riddell 203; Ken Welsh 211; Design Pics/The Irish Image Collection 215; Design Pics/Peter Zoeller 230–231.

Index

Achill Island 92
Adare 206
Anglo-Irish Treaty 13, 156
Anglo-Irish War 13, 156
Anglo-Normans 11–12
Antrim 19, 40–52
Aran Islands 201
Armagh 72, 74
Armagh City 73
Athlone Town 136

Ballykeel Dolmen 74
Battle of the Boyne 12
Beaghmore Stone Circles 78
Belfast 15, 52, 68
    City Hall 52
Ben Bulben 98
Ben Crom 68
Birr Castle 144
Booley Bay 192
Boru, Brian 11
burial chamber and
    standing stone 140
burial site of Samuel
    Grubb 248

Cahir Castle 210
Carrick-a-Rede 48
Castle Island 112
Cavan 72
Celts 11, 120
Christ Church Cathedral 164

Clare 202
Classiebawn Castle 94
Cliffs of Moher 201, 202
Clonmacnoise, abbey at 144
Coast 94, 110, 170
Cobh Cathedral 244
Connacht north 90–107
Connacht south 108–31
Connemara 120–24
Cookstown 78
Cork 236–244
County Antrim 40–52
County Armagh 74
County Cavan 72
County Clare 200, 202
County Cork 4, 236–244, 248
County Donegal 20–31, 202
County Down 52–69
County Dublin 148–167
County Fermanagh 86
County Galway 116–28
County Kerry 220–32
County Kildare 176
County Kilkenny 188
County Laois 172
County Leitrim 102
County Limerick 206
County Londonderry 32–36
County Louth 134
County Mayo 92
County Meath 134, 140
County Monaghan 86

County Offaly 144
County Roscommon 112–16
County Sligo 94–102
County Tipperary 206–14
County Tyrone 78–82
County Waterford 244–52
County Westmeath 136
County Wexford 192–96
County Wicklow 176–84
Crawfordsburn Country
    Park 60
Cromwell, Oliver 12, 102, 112, 240
Cromwell's Army 206
Custom House 160

Dail, the 160
Deenish and Scariff
    Islands 224
Derryclare Lough 120
Derrynane Bay 224
Devenish Island 86
Dingle 3, 220
    Peninsula 220
Doagh Famine
    Village 20
Dogs Bay 124
Donegal 20–28
Down 52–69
Dublin 148–67
Dublin Castle 156
Dun Aengus Fort 128
Dunagree Point 20

Dungarvan 248
Dunguaire Castle 128
Dunluce Castle 40
Dunseverick Castle 44

Easter Uprising 13
English Reformation 12
Enniskillen Castle 82
European Union 14, 124

Fanad Peninsula 24–28
Fermanagh 15, 82, 86
Folk Museum 24
Four Courts 156
Freud, Sigmund 14

Gaeltacht regions 14, 24
Galley Head 240
Galway 116–31
Galway City 111, 124
Garinish Island 236
Giant's Causeway 44
Glencar Waterfall 106
Glens of Antrim 48
Glencolumbkille 24
Glendalough 184
government buildings 160
Graiguenamanagh 188
Guildhall 32

Ha'penny Bridge 164
Henry VIII 12

Heywood Gardens 172
Hillsborough Castle 60
Hilton Park 86
Holy Cross Abbey 214
Home Rule Act 13
Hook Head 196
Hook Peninsula 192

Inishmore 128
Inishmurray Island 94
Inishowen 20
Irish Free State 13
Irish Republican Army
    (IRA) 13

Kerry 220–35
    Peninsula 220
    Ring of 224–228
Kildare 176
Kilkenny 12, 171
Kilkenny Castle 188
Kilmore Quay 2192
Knockmealdown
    Mountains 248
Kylemore 116

lake 72, 92, 112
Laois 172
Leinster north 132–67
Leinster south 168–97
Leitrim 102, 106
lily pool and temple 116
Limerick 206
Lismore Castle 244
Londonderry 32–36
Londonderry City 32

Lough Currane 224
Lough Foyle 20
Lough Gill 98
Lough Key Forest
    Park 112
Louth 134
Lower Lough Erne 86
Lugnaquilla 184

MacCul, Fionn 10, 44, 98
Markree Castle 102
Maynooth College 176
Meath 15, 134
Millisle 52
Moate 136
Monaghan 86
monastic ruins 94
Mount Stewart House 56
Mourne Mountains 64
Mullaghmore 94
Mulroy Bay 28
Munster north 198–215
Munster south 216–253
Mussenden Temple 36

Newcastle 64
Newgrange 140
Newtownards 56
Northern Ireland 10, 13–15

O'Connell Street 148, 152
Offaly 144
Omagh 78

Parkes Castle 102
Plantations policy 12, 14, 172

pleached lime alley 172
Portrush 40
Portsalon 24
Portstewart 36
potato famine 13, 20
Poulnabrone 202
Powerscourt Gardens 180

Rathmullan 28
Reconciliation Monument 32
Republic of Ireland 10, 13–14
River Barrow 188
River Garavogue 98
River Liffey 148, 176
River Shannon 136
Rock of Cashel 206
Roscommon 15, 64
Roundstone 124

Sackville Street 152
St Finan's Bay 224
St Joseph's Square 176
St Patrick's Cathedral 74
Scrabo Tower 56
sculpture of Jim Larkin
    and the Spire 148
Shannon 136
Shaw, George Bernard 10, 128, 228
Silent Valley 68
Slea Head 220
Slieve League 15, 19, 202
Sligo 94–103
Sligo City 98
Sneem 228
    Sculpture Park 228
Sperrin Mountains 78

Spire, the 148
Spraoi Festival 252
standing stone 140
statutes of Kilkenny 12
Stradbally 172
Strokestown Park 116
Swiss Cottage, the 210

temple 116
Thurles 214
Tipperary 200, 248
Torc Waterfall 232
traditional pub 136
Trim 135
Trim Castle 140
Trinity College 152
Twelve Pins 120
Tyrone 78, 82

Ulster History Park 78
Ulster north 16–69
Ulster south 70–89

Vikings 11
waterfall 60, 106, 232
Waterford 4, 11, 196, 248–252
Waterford City 252
Waterville 224
Westmeath 134
Wexford 192, 196
Wicklow 176–84
Wicklow Mountains 180, 184
Wilde, Oscar 10
windmill 52

Yeats, W.B. 10